Animals and the Environment
Snakes

Cobras

by Linda George

Content Consultants:

Donal M. Boyer
Associate Curator
Reptile Department
San Diego Zoo

"Bayou" Bob Popplewell,
Brazos Snake Ranch
Santo, Texas

CAPSTONE
HIGH/LOW BOOKS
an imprint of Capstone Press

C A P S T O N E   P R E S S

818 North Willow Street • Mankato, Minnesota 56001
http://www.capstone-press.com

Library of Congress Cataloging-in-Publication Data
George, Linda.
    Cobras/by Linda George.
    p. cm.--(Animals and the environment)
    Includes bibliographical references (p. 44) and index.
    Summary: Describes the physical characteristics, habitat, and behavior
of cobras.
ISBN 1-56065-691-3
    1. Cobras--Juvenile literature. [1. Cobras 2. Poisonous snakes. 3. Snakes.]
I. Title. II. Series: Animals & the environment.
QL666.O64G46   1998
597.96--dc21

                                                        97-31671
                                                          CIP
                                                           AC

Editorial credits:
Editor, Matt Doeden; cover design, Timothy Halldin; illustrations,
    James Franklin; photo research, Michelle L. Norstad
Photo credits:
Root Resources/Claudia Adams, 8; A.B. Sheldon, 43
Unicorn Stock/Russell R. Grundke, cover
Visuals Unlimited/Joe McDonald, 6, 12, 14, 17, 18, 22, 26, 32, 35, 36, 46;
    Milton H. Tierney, 11; Ken Lucas, 21; Max and Bea Hunn, 25;
    Jim Merli, 29, 30, 40-41; D. Cavagnaro, 39

Table of Contents

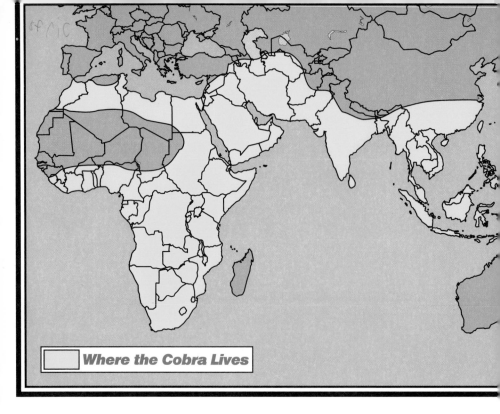

Where the Cobra Lives

Fast Facts about Cobras

Kinds: All cobras are Elapids. Elapids are venomous snakes with hollow teeth. Venom comes out of their teeth through small holes. Venom is a poisonous liquid produced by some animals.

Range: Cobras live in India, southern China, Africa, the Middle East, and southeastern Asia.

4

Description: Cobras come in many colors. Some cobras have colored bands and markings on their bodies. Most cobras are five to 18 feet (1.5 to 5.5 meters) long. Shield-nosed cobras are smaller. Shield-nosed cobras are only 30 inches (76 centimeters) long.

Habits: Cobras raise their heads when they sense danger. Some cobras spread the bones in their necks to form hoods.

Food: Cobras eat mice, small birds, frogs, fish, and other snakes. King cobras eat mostly other snakes.

Mating: Different kinds of cobras mate at different times of the year. Usually, cobra females lay 20 to 50 eggs.

Life Span: Cobras live up to 20 years.

Living Area: Cobras live in grasslands, woodlands, plains, rocky hillsides, and forests. They usually live near water.

Chapter 1
About Cobras

Cobras are in the family Elapidae. A family is a group of animals with similar characteristics. Snakes in this family have hollow fangs. A fang is a long, sharp tooth. A fang has a hole at the tip so venom can pass through it. Venom is a poisonous liquid produced by some animals.

Some cobras spread the bones in their necks when they sense danger. This makes their necks look like hoods. Cobras usually show their hoods before biting. Cobras bite humans only when the snakes cannot escape.

Some cobras spread the bones in their necks when they sense danger.

Most adult cobras are five to 18 feet (1.5 to 5.5 meters) long. Adult shield-nosed cobras are only 30 inches (76 centimeters) long. Cobras live in southeasterm Asia, India, southern China, Africa, and the Middle East. Cobras do not live in North America.

Cobras usually live in holes in the ground. Some live in trees or rock piles. During the day, most cobras stay in rocky areas. They rest under bushes and rocks. Cobras move between the sun and shade to keep their body temperatures within a comfortable range.

Snake Charmers

Many people think of snake charmers when they think of cobras. Snake charmers play flutes as cobras rise out of baskets. Snake charmers' cobras appear to hear the music.

But cobras are not really charmed by music. Snakes are deaf. They have no eardrums. Cobras rise out of baskets because the

Many people think of snake charmers when they think of cobras.

charmers move their flutes. The cobras see the movement as danger. They rise and show their hoods. Snake charmers sit far enough away so cobras cannot bite.

Deadly Venom

Cobras have special glands behind their eyes. Cobras use muscles to squeeze these glands when they release venom. Venom comes out through fangs in the top of cobras' mouths.

Cobras use their venom in two ways. All cobras squeeze venom through their fangs. Some cobras can also spit venom at victims' eyes. The venom causes pain, blurred sight, and dizziness. Victims must wash venom from their eyes quickly. If they do not, they might go blind.

Cobra venom kills quickly if it enters the blood of their victims. Humans can die from cobra venom in 15 minutes. But venom usually takes longer to kill people.

Cobra Senses

Cobras sense mainly through smell and taste. Cobras use their tongues to smell and taste the air

Cobras use their tongues to smell and taste the air around them.

around them. They flick their tongues out every few seconds to do this. Cobras rub their tongues against their Jacobson's organs. The Jacobson's organs are tiny sacs on the top of cobras' mouths. They are special taste detectors. Cobras use their noses only for breathing.

Cobras cannot hear. But some cobras have good vision. They use their vision to hunt.

Chapter 2
Cobra Defenses

Cobras can release deadly venom when they bite. But biting is not the only way cobras defend themselves. Some cobras play dead when they sense danger. Others spit at their enemies. Most cobras show their hoods to warn enemies. Cobras usually try to escape danger if they are given the chance.

Playing Dead
Most predators will not eat dead animals. Some cobras lie very still if they are cornered.

Most cobras show their hoods to warn enemies.

Spitting cobras like this one spit venom at their enemies.

They lie on their backs with their tongues sticking out. This is called playing dead.

Small shield-nosed cobras often play dead when they sense danger. Black-necked spitting cobras and red spitting cobras also play dead. These cobras will remain still until they can escape. They might attack if they cannot escape.

14

Spitting

Some cobras spit or spray venom at their enemies. These cobras aim for their enemies' eyes. The venom causes pain, blurred sight, and dizziness. It can even cause blindness.

Some kinds of African and Asian cobras can spit venom. Some cobras can spit as far as 15 feet (4.5 meters).

Hoods

Almost all cobras have hoods. Cobras show their hoods when they sense danger. The hoods make the cobras look bigger than they really are. The hoods scare away animals and birds that want to eat cobras. Most cobras hiss as they show their hoods.

Indian cobras have the largest hoods. Their hoods are up to four times wider than their bodies. Some cobras like tree cobras don't have hoods.

Size

King cobras are the largest venomous snakes in the world. They use their size as a defense. Adult king cobras are 14 to 18 feet (4.2 to 5.5 meters) long.

King cobras can raise their heads five to six feet (1.5 to 1.8 meters) off the ground. That is about one-third of their total length. Some king cobras can make themselves taller than an average person. King cobra venom can kill an elephant in two or three hours.

King cobras are most likely to attack when they are surprised. They may also attack when they are guarding their eggs. Sometimes a king cobra nest is found near a village. Often everyone will leave the village until the young cobras hatch from the eggs.

King cobras are the largest venomous snakes in the world.

Chapter 3

Hunting and Striking

Cobras usually bite their prey as soon as they can. Prey is an animal hunted by another animal for food.

Cobras inject venom into their prey. They let go of their prey after they are done injecting venom. Prey often tries to escape.

A cobra usually bites its prey immediately.

But the cobra venom stops prey from going far. Within seconds, an animal injected with cobra venom cannot move.

What Cobras Eat

Cobras eat mice and small birds. Cobras also eat frogs, fish, and other water animals. Sometimes young cobras eat insects.

King cobras eat other snakes. King cobras often share their sleeping places with other snakes. But sometimes the king cobras wake up hungry. They may eat one or more of the snakes nearby.

Swallowing Food

Cobras eat prey that is still alive. Cobras swallow their prey whole. The bones in cobra jaws can open wide. This allows cobras to eat large prey. Cobras can swallow animals wider than their own heads.

King cobras eat other snakes.

Swallowing takes a long time. A cobra uses its fangs to grasp its prey's head. The cobra pulls the prey down its throat and into its stomach. The prey often struggles as it is swallowed.

Cobra Strikes

Cobras prepare to fight when they sense danger. They lift their heads off the ground. They show their hoods. They do this to frighten away enemies.

Sometimes cobras pretend to strike with their mouths closed. They do this to frighten away enemies. Cobras sometimes save their venom for hunting. They may bite but not release venom. These bites are called dry strikes.

Cobras lift their heads off the ground when they are in danger.

Treating Cobra Bites

Cobra bites can be treated with an antivenin. An antivenin is a medicine that reduces the effects of venom. Scientists use the chemicals in snake venom to make antivenin. Scientists give victims of cobra bites antivenin. Most victims must take antivenin in shots.

Extracting venom from a cobra is dangerous. Extract means to take out. Scientists must first capture a cobra. They hold it by the neck so it cannot bite.

Scientists hook a cobra's fangs over the edge of a jar. Venom comes out of the fangs and drips into the jar. Scientists call this milking a snake.

Scientists take venom from cobras to make antivenin.

Chapter 4
Mating

Cobras can mate when they are two or three years old. Mate means to join together to produce young. Different cobras mate at different times of the year.

Some cobras molt when mating season begins. Molt means to shed an outer layer of skin. Cobras grow a new layer of outer skin while they molt. Cobras also molt at other times during the year. Young cobras usually molt more often than older cobras.

Some cobras molt when mating season begins.

The skin over a molting snake's eyes turns white. The skin begins to peel away from the mouth. The snake wiggles out of the peeling skin. The old skin turns inside out. The snake leaves it behind.

Female cobras give off a scent when they molt. Male cobras smell the scent. The scent draws the males to the females.

Cobras mate when a male cobra finds a female. The male wraps his body around the female. The cobras may be wrapped together for hours.

King Cobra Nests

Female king cobras build nests after mating. Other cobras do not build nests. King cobras push dead leaves and rotting plants together. They usually build their nests on the forest floor.

A king cobra nest has two rooms. The female lays 20 to 50 eggs in one room. The

A group of cobra eggs is a clutch.

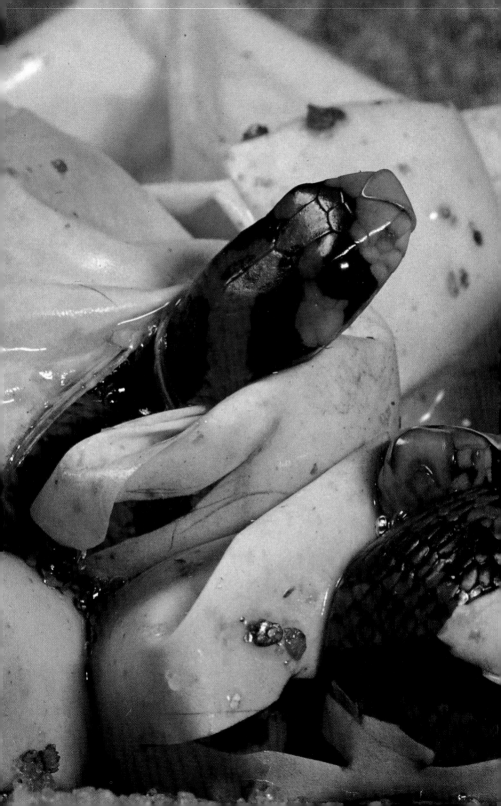

group of eggs is called a clutch. The female stays with the clutch.

The female guards against predators in the other room. Some predators like mongooses and monitor lizards eat cobra eggs.

Cobra Young

Young cobras hatch from eggs about 60 days after the eggs are laid. Young cobras are about 10 to 20 inches (25 to 51 centimeters) long. They are born with a supply of venom. Cobras that are just one hour old can already kill.

Adult cobras do not stay near their newly hatched young. They leave the nest as soon as the young hatch. Young cobras must care for themselves right away.

Young cobras hatch from eggs about 60 days after the eggs are laid.

Chapter 5

Cobras and People

Scientists believe that cobras have existed for more than 20 million years. Cobras are among the most widely recognized snakes in the world. They are also among the most deadly. Some scientists think cobras are also the smartest snakes.

Cobras are among the most widely recognized snakes in the world.

Meeting a Cobra

The only cobras in North America live in zoos. But cobras live in the wild in some parts of the world. People must stay away from common cobra sleeping places. Common cobra sleeping places are rocky areas, burrows, old buildings, and bushes near water.

People should never go near king cobra nests. King cobras are most likely to attack people who approach their nests.

A person faced with a cobra should stand still. Sudden movements can frighten the snake. A cobra needs plenty of room to escape. The best way to get away from a cobra is to back up slowly.

People should wear boots and loose pants when they are walking in cobra territory. Many cobra bites occur because people

Rocky areas are common cobra sleeping places.

accidentally step on or near cobras. Boots and pants might keep a cobra's fangs from touching a person's skin.

Buddha's Story

There is a story about how the Indian cobra got its markings. The Indian cobra has markings on the back of its head. The story is about a man named Buddha. Buddha lived long ago.

The story says Buddha fell asleep after a day's travel. When morning came, a cobra spread its hood to shade Buddha. Buddha was thankful for the cobra's shade. He blessed the snake and put his fingers on its hood. The story says this left the marks seen today.

A story says that the Indian cobra got its markings from a man named Buddha.

The Future of Cobras

Some of the cobras' range has been destroyed. There are fewer cobras now than there once were because of this. But the cobra is not in danger of becoming extinct. Extinct means no longer living anywhere in the world.

Some people hunt cobras. They kill cobras because the snakes are venomous. Others kill cobras to sell their skins. Cobra skins are valuable. Cobra skins can sell for hundreds of dollars each.

The governments of some countries are protecting cobras. India's government controls how many cobra skins can be sold. It is against the law to kill cobras in Egypt. Countries that protect cobras help cobras survive in nature.

A cobra skin can sell for hundreds of dollars.

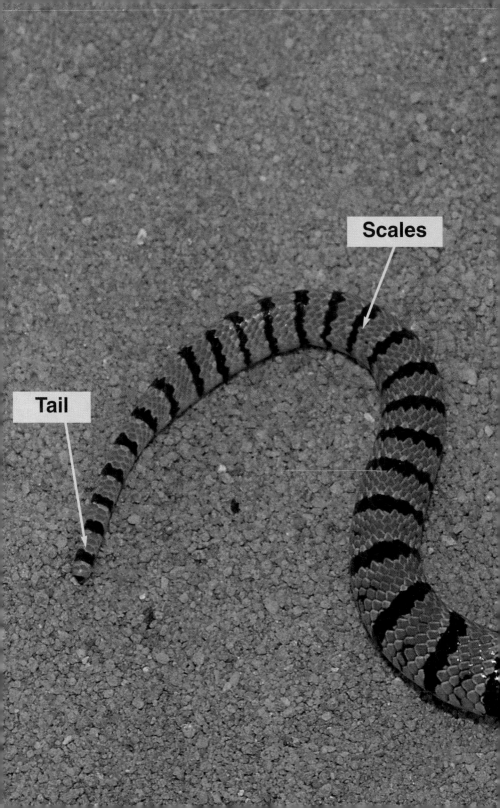

Scales

Tail

Head

Hood

Band Markings

Words to Know

antivenin (an-tee-VEN-in)—a medicine that reduces the effects of snake poison

clutch (KLUHCH)—a group of eggs

dry strike (DRYE STRIKE)—a venomless snake bite

extinct (ek-STINGKT)—no longer living anywhere in the world

extract (ek-STRAKT)—to take out

fang (FANG)—a long, sharp tooth; venom passes through it.

mate (MATE)—to join together to produce young

molt (MOHLT)—to shed an outer layer of skin

predator (PRED-uh-tur)—an animal that hunts and eats other animals

prey (PRAY)—an animal hunted by another animal for food

venom (VEN-uhm)—a poisonous liquid produced by some animals

To Learn More

Ethan, Eric. *Cobras.* Milwaukee, Wisconsin: Gareth Stevens Publishing, 1995.

Gerholdt, James E. *King Cobras.* Edina, Minn: Abdo & Daughters, 1996.

Grace, Eric S. *Snakes.* San Francisco: Sierra Club Books for Children, 1994.

Martin, James. *The Spitting Cobras of Africa.* Minneapolis: Capstone Press, 1995.

Useful Addresses

Metropolitan Toronto Zoo
West Hill
Box 280
Toronto, ON M1D 4R5
Canada

National Zoological Park
3001 Connecticut Avenue NW
Washington, DC 20008

**Society for the Study of Amphibians
 and Reptiles**
P.O. Box 626
Hays, KS 67601-0626

Internet Sites

Cobra Information Site
http://www.livenet.net/~cobra/index.htm

Learn About Snakes!
http://www.mvhs.srvusd.k12.ca.us/~shayati/think.
  html

The Snake Page
http://www.geocities.com/CapeCanaveral/4538/

Index